.Y

Daily Reflections

EDITED BY
Alberto Rossa, CMF

Novalis
Toronto, Canada

Paulist Press
New York / Mahwah, NJ

The quotations in this book are from writings and talks of Pope Francis and are used by permission of Libreria Editrice Vaticana. All rights reserved.

Originally published by Claretian Publications, Macao
PO Box 1608 Macao, SAR, China
www.bibleclaret.org

This English edition published by Paulist Press
997 Macarthur Boulevard
Mahwah, NJ 07430
www.paulistpress.com

Cover image by CNS photo / Paul Haring. Used with permission.
Cover and book design by Lynn Else

Library of Congress Cataloging-in-Publication Data is available upon request.

ISBN 978-0-8091-4948-3 (paperback)
ISBN 978-1-58768-572-9 (e-book)

Published in Canada by Novalis
Publishing Office
10 Lower Spadina Ave., Suite 400
Toronto, Ontario, Canada
M5V 2Z2
www.novalis.ca

Head Office
4475 Frontenac St.
Montreal, Quebec, Canada
H2H 2S2

ISBN: 978-2-89688-249-6

Printed and bound in Canada

Contents

Opening Prayer v

January 1

February 35

March 65

April 99

May 131

June 165

July 197

August 231

September 265

October 297

November 331

December 363

Prayer for the Year of the Family 396

Opening Prayer

Let us fervently call upon Mary Most Holy, the Mother of Jesus and our Mother, and Saint Joseph, her spouse. Let us ask them to enlighten, comfort, and guide every family in the world, so that they may fulfill with dignity and peace the mission which God has entrusted to them.

Holy Family of Nazareth,
grant that our families too
may be places of communion and prayer,
authentic schools of the Gospel,
and small domestic churches.

Holy Family of Nazareth,
may families never again
experience violence, rejection, and division:
may all who have been hurt or scandalized
find ready comfort and healing.

(Angelus Message, December 29, 2013)

January

Jesus, Mary, and Joseph

Behold, children are a heritage from the LORD, the fruit of the womb a reward. Like arrows in the hand of a warrior are the children of one's youth. Blessed is the man who fills his quiver with them! He shall not be put to shame when he speaks with his enemies in the gate.

Psalm 127:3–5

Jesus is the incarnation of the
Living God, the one who brings life
amid so many deeds of death,
amid sin, selfishness, and
self-absorption. Jesus accepts,
loves, uplifts, encourages,
forgives, restores
the ability to walk,
gives back life.

Jesus is rich in the same way
as a child who feels loved
and who loves its parents,
without doubting their
love and tenderness
for an instant.

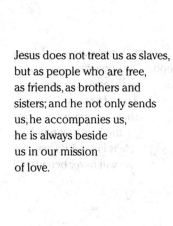

Jesus does not treat us as slaves,
but as people who are free,
as friends, as brothers and
sisters; and he not only sends
us, he accompanies us,
he is always beside
us in our mission
of love.

Never forget the gaze of Jesus
upon you; upon you, upon you…
never forget his gaze! It is a
gaze of love. And thus you
shall be forever certain of
the Lord's faithful love.
He is faithful. Be assured:
he will never betray you!

With a tenderness that never
disappoints but is always
capable of restoring our joy,
Jesus makes it possible
for us to lift up our heads
and to start anew.

The Magi's example helps us to lift our gaze toward the star and to follow the great desires of our heart. They teach us not to be content with a life of mediocrity, of "playing it safe," but to let ourselves be attracted always by what is good, true, and beautiful... by God, who is all of this, and so much more!

Ours is not a joy born of having many possessions, but from having encountered a Person: Jesus, in our midst; it is born from knowing that with him we are never alone, even at difficult moments, even when our life's journey comes up against problems and obstacles that seem insurmountable, and there are so many of them!

Jesus has shown us that the face of God is that of a loving Father. Sin and death have been defeated. Christians cannot be pessimists! They do not look like someone in constant mourning. If we are truly in love with Christ and if we sense how much he loves us, our heart will "light up" with a joy that spreads to everyone around us.

Jesus, the Good Shepherd,
does not humiliate or abandon
people to remorse. Through him
the tenderness of the Father, who
consoles and revitalizes, speaks;
it is he who brings us from the
disintegration of shame—because
shame truly breaks us up—
to the fabric of trust; he restores
courage, re-entrusts responsibility,
and sends us out on mission.

Only if you have a personal
encounter with Jesus can you be
an instrument for others to
encounter him.

In every Eucharistic celebration, Jesus offers himself for us to the Father, so that we too can be united with him, offering to God our lives, our work, our joys, and our sorrows…offering everything as a spiritual sacrifice.

It is for the Christian to continually encounter Jesus, to watch him, to let himself be watched over by Jesus because Jesus watches us with love; he loves us so much, he loves us so much and he is always watching over us.

Remember this always: faith is
walking with Jesus; and it is a walk
that lasts a lifetime. At the end, there
shall be the definitive encounter.
Certainly, at some moments on the
journey, we feel tired and confused.
But the faith gives us the certainty
of Jesus' constant presence in every
situation, even the most painful or
difficult to understand.

When one finds Jesus, that person is captivated, overcome, and it is a joy to leave our usual lifestyle, sometimes desolate and apathetic, to embrace the Gospel, to let ourselves be guided by the new logic of love and of humble and unselfish service.

Our people are tired of words; they don't need teachers so much as they need witnesses. And witnesses gain inner strength through an encounter with Jesus Christ.

I invite all Christians, everywhere, at
this very moment, to a renewed
personal encounter with Jesus
Christ, or at least an openness to
letting him encounter them; I ask
all of you to do this unfailingly
each day. No one should think that
this invitation is not meant for him
or her, since "no one is excluded
from the joy brought by the Lord."

The Lord does not disappoint those
who take this risk; whenever we
take a step toward Jesus, we come
to realize that he is already there,
waiting for us with open arms.

If you adore Christ and walk
behind him and with him, your
diocesan Church and your parishes
will grow in faith and in charity,
in the joy of evangelizing. You'll be
a Church in which fathers,
mothers, priests, men and women
religious, catechists, children, old
and young people walk alongside
each other, support each other,
help each other, love each other
like brothers and sisters,
especially in difficult times.

Following Jesus means deciding to walk in his footsteps, and that guarantees the cross. Such a path is far removed from the concessions made by those whose divided hearts dream of peaceful harmony between the Lord of glory and the spirit of the world!

Today Christ is knocking at the
door of your heart, of my heart.
He calls you and me to rise, to be
wide awake and alert, and to see
the things in life that really matter.
What is more, he is asking you and
me to go out on the highways
and byways of this world, knocking
on the doors of other people's
hearts, inviting them to welcome
him into their lives.

Mary grew up in the home of Joachim and Anne…surrounded by their love and faith: in their home she learned to listen to the Lord and to follow his will. Saints Joachim and Anne were part of a long chain of people who had transmitted their faith and love for God…in the warmth and love of family life, down to Mary, who received the Son of God in her womb and who gave him to the world, to us.

As mother of all, Mary is a sign of hope for peoples suffering the birth pangs of justice. She is the missionary who draws near to us and accompanies us throughout life, opening our hearts to faith by her maternal love. As a true mother, she walks at our side, she shares our struggles, and she constantly surrounds us with God's love.

Mary was able to turn a stable
into a home for Jesus, with poor
swaddling clothes and an
abundance of love. She is the
handmaid of the Father who sings
his praises. She is the friend who is
ever concerned that wine not be
lacking in our lives. She is the
woman whose heart was
pierced by a sword and who
understands all our pain.

May we never fail to experience the
affection and tenderness of Mary,
who whispers in our ears the Word
of God in familiar language.
Hearing that, we will have the
strength to resist the sweet talk
of the Evil One and disdain
his enticements.

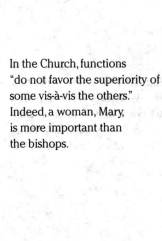

In the Church, functions
"do not favor the superiority of
some vis-à-vis the others."
Indeed, a woman, Mary,
is more important than
the bishops.

There is a Marian "style" to the
Church's work of evangelization.
Whenever we look to Mary,
we come to believe once again
in the revolutionary nature
of love and tenderness.

Along our path, which is often
difficult, we are not alone. We are
so many, we are a people, and the
gaze of Our Lady helps us to look at
one another as brothers and sisters.
Let us look upon one another
in a more fraternal way! Mary
teaches us to have that gaze
that strives to welcome, to
accompany, and to protect.

Joseph was following a good life
plan, but God had a different
design for him, a greater mission.
Joseph was a man who always
listened to the voice of God,
profoundly amenable to God's
secret will, a man attentive
to the messages that came
from the depths of the
heart and from above.

As the spouse of Mary, he (Joseph) is at her side in good times and bad, on the journey to Bethlehem for the census and in the anxious and joyful hours when she gave birth; amid the drama of the flight into Egypt and during the frantic search for their child in the Temple; and later in the day-to-day life of the home of Nazareth, in the workshop where he taught his trade to Jesus.

In the Gospels, Saint Joseph appears as a strong and courageous man, a working man, yet in his heart we see great tenderness, which is not the virtue of the weak but rather a sign of strength of spirit and a capacity for concern, for compassion, for genuine openness to others, for love. We must not be afraid of goodness, of tenderness!

The angel of the Lord revealed to
Joseph the dangers that threatened
Jesus and Mary, forcing them
to flee to Egypt and then to
settle in Nazareth. So too,
in our time, God calls upon us
to recognize the dangers
threatening our own
families and to protect
them from harm.

February

*The Sacrament of Marriage:
Journeying Together*

So faith, hope, and love remain,
these three; but the greatest of
these is love.

1 Corinthians 13:13

It is as though matrimony were first a human sacrament, where the person discovers himself, understands himself in relation to others and in a relationship of love which is capable of receiving and giving.

In marriage, we give ourselves completely without calculation or reserve, sharing everything, gifts and hardship, trusting in God's Providence. This is the experience that the young can learn from their parents and grandparents. It is an experience of faith in God and of mutual trust, profound freedom and holiness, because holiness presumes giving oneself with fidelity and sacrifice every day of one's life!

God's love becomes present
and active by the way
of love and by the good
works that we do.

Two Christians who marry have recognized the call of the Lord in their own love story, the vocation to form one flesh and one life from two, male and female. And the Sacrament of Holy Matrimony envelops this love in the grace of God, it roots it in God himself. By this gift, and by the certainty of this call, you can continue on assured; you have nothing to fear; you can face everything together!

It is important to dream and to dream in the family. Please, don't lose this ability to dream in this way. How many solutions are found to family problems if we take the time to reflect—if we think of our husband or wife and we dream about the good qualities that they have? Don't ever lose the illusion of when you were boyfriend and girlfriend.

This is what marriage is all about:
man and woman walking together,
wherein the husband helps his wife
to become ever more a woman,
and wherein the woman has the
task of helping her husband to
become ever more a man.

In the course of salvation history, matrimony has been conceived in terms of family descent and a people's history. It is based on a command of God that is repeated frequently in the New Testament.

Jesus is he who brings generations closer. He is the font of that love which unites families and people, conquering all diffidence, all isolation, all distance. This causes us to also think of grandparents: how important their presence is, the presence of grandparents! How precious their role is in the family and in society!

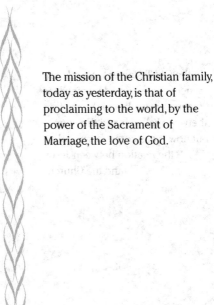

The mission of the Christian family, today as yesterday, is that of proclaiming to the world, by the power of the Sacrament of Marriage, the love of God.

In the Old Testament, the relation
between man and woman was
seen as a symbol of the relation
between Yahweh and the people,
but now it has come to symbolize
the relation between Jesus
and the Church.

Grace is not given to decorate life
but rather to make us strong in life,
giving us courage to go forward!
And without isolating oneself but
always staying together. Christians
celebrate the sacrament of
marriage because they know
they need it! They need it to
stay together and to carry out
their mission as parents....
*"In joy and in sadness,
in sickness and in health."*

Those who celebrate the sacrament say, *"I promise to be true to you, in joy and in sadness, in sickness and in health; I will love you and honor you all the days of my life."* At that moment, the couple does not know what will happen, or what joys and pains await them. They are setting out, like Abraham, on a journey together. And that is what marriage is! Setting out and walking together....Hand in hand, always and for the rest of their lives.

There are problems in marriage:
always different points of view,
jealousy, arguing. But we need to
say to young spouses that they
should never end the day without
making peace. The Sacrament of
marriage is renewed in this act of
peace after an argument, a
misunderstanding, a hidden
jealousy, even a sin.

Sacramental marriage is a gift of God as well as a commitment. The love of two spouses is sanctified by Christ, and a married couple is called to bear witness to and cultivate this sanctity through their faithful love for one another.

At a time of great crisis for family life—as we are all aware—our Christian communities are called to support married couples and families in fulfilling their proper mission in the life of the Church and society. The family remains the basic unit of society and the first school in which children learn the human, spiritual, and moral values that enable them to be a beacon of goodness, integrity, and justice in our communities.

The holiness and indissolubility
of Christian matrimony,
often disintegrating under
tremendous pressure from the
secular world, must be deepened
by clear doctrine and supported
by the witness of committed
married couples.

Christian matrimony is a lifelong covenant of love between one man and one woman; it entails real sacrifices in order to turn away from illusory notions of sexual freedom and in order to foster conjugal fidelity.

Spousal and familial love also clearly reveals the vocation of the person to love in a unique way and forever, and that the trials, sacrifices, and crises of couples, as well as of the family as a whole, represent pathways for growth in goodness, truth, and beauty.

Married life must be persevering because otherwise love cannot go forward. Perseverance in love, in good times and in difficult times, when there are problems: problems with the children, economic problems, problems here, problems there—but love perseveres, presses on, always trying to work things out, to save the family.

Let us think about our parents,
about our grandparents, and great
grandparents: they married in
much poorer conditions than our
own. Some married during wartime
or just after a war. Some, like my
own parents, emigrated. Where did
they find the strength? They found
it in the certainty that the Lord was
with them, that their families were
blessed by God through the
Sacrament of Matrimony.

"In joy and in sadness, in sickness and in health." This is what the spouses say to one another during the celebration of the sacrament, and in their marriage, they pray with one another and with the community. Why? Because it is helpful to do so? No! They do so because they need to, for the long journey they are making together: it is a long journey, not for a brief spell but for an entire life!

In a marriage, fertility can sometimes be put to the test when the children do not arrive or are sick....In such times of trial, there are couples who look to Jesus and draw on the power of fertility that Christ has with his Church.

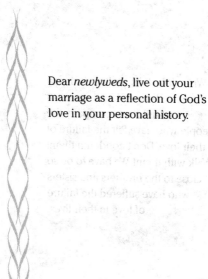

Dear *newlyweds*, live out your marriage as a reflection of God's love in your personal history.

When love fails, and it fails many
times, we have to feel the pain of
that failure, accompany the
people who have felt the failure of
their love. Don't condemn them!
Walk with them! We have to be so
close to the brothers and sisters
who have suffered the failure
of love in their lives.

Familial love is fruitful…not only
because it generates new lives,
but also because it broadens the
horizon of existence, it creates a
new world; it makes us believe,
despite any discouragement and
defeatism, that coexistence based
on respect and trust is possible.

A family can become a blessing to the world. God's love becomes present and active by the way of love and by the good works that we do. We extend Christ's kingdom in this world. And in doing this, we prove faithful to the prophetic mission which we have received in baptism.

The restlessness of love is always an
incentive to go toward the other,
without waiting for the other to
manifest his need.

The family is also threatened by
growing efforts on the part of some
to redefine the very institution of
marriage, by relativism, by the
culture of the ephemeral, by a
lack of openness to life.

March

Suffering and Family Burdens

God's Mercy and Forgiveness

The Cross

But from everlasting to everlasting
the LORD's love is with those who
fear him, and his righteousness
with their children's children.

Psalm 103:17

Let us also think of the other "exiles": I would call them "hidden exiles," those exiles who can be found within their own families: the elderly, for example, who are sometimes treated as a burdensome presence.

Let us approach with care and affection those families who are struggling, forced to leave their homeland, broken, homeless or unemployed, or suffering for any reason; let us approach married couples in crisis or separated.

We see signs of an idolatry of
wealth, power, and pleasure which
come at a high cost to human lives.
Closer to home, so many of our
own friends and contemporaries,
even in the midst of immense
material prosperity, are suffering
from spiritual poverty, loneliness,
and quiet despair.

We cannot ignore the hardship
of many families due to
unemployment, the problem of
housing, the suffering due to
internal conflicts within families,
to the failures of the conjugal and
family experience, and to the
violence that lurks in families,
wreaking havoc in homes.
We…wish to be particularly close
to them with respect and with a
true sense of solidarity.

We want above all to remember the simple but beautiful and brave testimony of so many families who joyfully live the experience of marriage and parenthood enlightened and sustained by the Lord's grace and fearlessly face even moments of the cross. Lived in union with the cross of the Lord, the cross does not hinder the path of love but, on the contrary, can make it stronger and fuller.

Certain silences are oppressive,
even at times within families,
between husbands and wives,
between parents and children,
among siblings. Without love, the
burden becomes even heavier,
intolerable. I think of elderly people
living alone and families who
receive no help in caring for
someone at home with special
needs. *"Come to me, all who labor
and are heavy laden,"* Jesus says.

Sadly, in this world, with all its highly developed technology, great numbers of children continue to live in inhuman situations, on the fringes of society, in the peripheries of great cities, and in the countryside.

There is no place for the elderly or for the unwanted child; there is no time for that poor person in the street. At times, it seems that for some people, human relations are regulated by two modern "dogmas": efficiency and pragmatism.

The message that comes from the
Holy Family is first of all a message
of faith. In the family life of Mary
and Joseph, God is truly at the
center, and he is so in the Person of
Jesus. This is why the Family of
Nazareth is holy. Why? Because it
is centered on Jesus.

Families will always have their
trials, but you may never add to
them. Instead, be living examples
of love, forgiveness, and care.
Be sanctuaries of respect for life,
proclaiming the sacredness
of every human life from
conception to natural death.

Hopelessness causes families to disintegrate. David was given the mission of uniting the people of God, but his impatience led him to destroy the family, the basic unit of the people.

If you go to him with your whole life, even with the many sins, instead of reproaching you, he will rejoice: this is our Father. This you must say, say it to many people, today. Whoever experiences divine mercy is impelled to be an architect of mercy among the least and the poor.

The wisdom of our grandparents is
the inheritance we ought to
receive. A people that does not
care for its grandparents, that
does not respect its grandparents,
has no future since it has lost
its memory.

Adultery has always been considered a grave sin, even if only desired. It has been punished severely because it was seen as comparable to violating the covenant. Thus, Israel differed from other cultures and religions in giving adultery a public dimension; it was seen as offending not only against the private institution of matrimony but also against divine law.

When we are unfaithful, we usually
betray not just ideas but concrete
persons. We take leave of those
who taught us the faith, those
who trained us well, those who
remain faithful to the Lord.

The one who brought us Jesus is a woman. It is the way that Jesus chose. He wanted to have a mother: even the gift of faith passes through women....

You can't have a family without dreams. Once a family loses the ability to dream, children do not grow, love does not grow, life shrivels up and dies....Dreaming is very important....Do not lose this ability to dream!

Let us remember this in our lives as Christians: God always waits for us, even when we have left him behind! He is never far from us, and if we return to him, he is ready to embrace us.

The gift of the Holy Family was entrusted to Saint Joseph so that he could care for it. Each of you, each of us—for I too am part of a family—is charged with caring for God's plan. The angel of the Lord revealed to Joseph the dangers which threatened Jesus and Mary, forcing them to flee to Egypt and then to settle in Nazareth. So too, in our time, God calls upon us to recognize the dangers threatening our own families and to protect them from harm.

God's patience has to call forth in
us the courage to return to him,
however many mistakes and sins
there may be in our life.

And this is important! To know how to forgive one another in families because we all make mistakes, all of us! Sometimes we do things which are not good and which harm others. It is important to have the courage to ask for forgiveness when we are at fault in the family.

It is the task of the wise
to recognize errors,
to feel pain, to repent,
to beg for pardon,
and to cry.

Perhaps each one of us feels troubled in his heart, perhaps he experiences darkness in his heart, perhaps he feels a little sad over a fault....He has come to take away all of this. He gives us peace, he forgives everything.

Let us listen to the cry of all those
who are weeping, who are
suffering, and who are dying
because of violence, terrorism,
or war in the Holy Land, so dear
to Saint Francis,…throughout
the Middle East and
everywhere in the world.

Let us ask the Lord for the grace to weep over our indifference, to weep over the cruelty of our world, of our own hearts, and of all those who in anonymity make social and economic decisions which open the door to tragic situations like this. "Has anyone wept?" Today has anyone wept in our world?

The Lord never tires of forgiving:
never! It is we who tire of asking his
forgiveness. Let us ask for the grace
not to tire of asking forgiveness
because he never tires of forgiving.
Let us ask for this grace.

Let everyone be moved to look into
the depths of his or her conscience
and listen to that word which says,
leave behind the self-interest that
hardens your heart, overcome the
indifference that makes your heart
insensitive toward others, conquer
your deadly reasoning, and open
yourself to dialogue and
reconciliation.

I want to mention now two attitudes that clearly reveal that a person has assumed the Lord's mission on the cross. The two attitudes are apostolic courage and constancy, and they go together.

The cross is what marks out the militant dimension of our existence. With the cross, it is impossible to negotiate, impossible to dialogue: the cross is either embraced or rejected. If we decide to reject it, our life will remain trapped in our own hands, encased in the petty confines of our short horizons.

If we embrace the cross, then by
that very decision we lose our life;
we leave it in the hands of God,
in the time of God, and it will
be given back to us in
a different form.

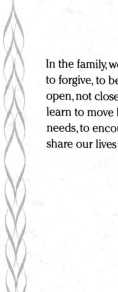

In the family, we learn how to love, to forgive, to be generous and open, not closed and selfish. We learn to move beyond our own needs, to encounter others and share our lives with them.

April

Peace, Joy, Hope

Honor your father and your mother, so that you may live long in the land the LORD your God is giving you.

Exodus 20:12

April

From the heart of the person renewed in the likeness of God comes good behavior: to speak always the truth and avoid all deceit; not to steal, but rather to share all you have with others, especially those in need; not to give in to anger, resentment, and revenge, but to be meek, magnanimous, and ready to forgive; not to gossip which ruins the good name of people, but to look more at the good side of everyone.

Washing one another's feet signifies welcoming, accepting, loving, and serving one another. It means serving the poor, the sick, and the outcast, those whom I find difficult, those who annoy me.

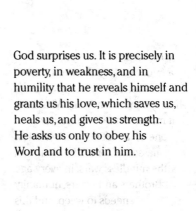

God surprises us. It is precisely in poverty, in weakness, and in humility that he reveals himself and grants us his love, which saves us, heals us, and gives us strength. He asks us only to obey his Word and to trust in him.

With the heart of a son, a brother,
a father, I ask each of you, indeed
for all of us, to have a conversion of
heart: to move on from "What does
it matter to me?" to tears for each
one of the fallen of… "senseless
massacre," for all the victims of
the mindless wars, in every age.
Brothers and sisters, humanity
needs to weep, and this
is the time to weep.

Christ's resurrection everywhere
calls forth seeds of that new world;
even if they are cut back, they grow
again, for the resurrection is
already secretly woven into the
fabric of this history, for Jesus did
not rise in vain. May we never
remain on the sidelines of this
march of living hope!

We adore God who is love, who in Jesus Christ gave himself for us, offered himself on the Cross to atone for our sins, and by the power of this love, rose from the dead and lives in his Church.

Let us not flee from the resurrection of Jesus, let us never give up, come what will. May nothing inspire more than his life, which impels us onward!

When a person truly knows Jesus Christ and believes in him, that person experiences Jesus' presence in life as well as the power of his Resurrection....One cannot but communicate this experience.

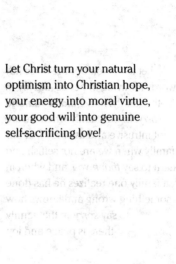

Let Christ turn your natural
optimism into Christian hope,
your energy into moral virtue,
your good will into genuine
self-sacrificing love!

Let us remember the three key words for living in peace and joy in the family: *may I*, *thank you*, and *sorry*. In our family when we are not intrusive and ask *may I*, in our family when we are not selfish and learn to say *thank you*, and when in a family one realizes he has done something wrong and knows how to say *sorry*, in that family there is peace and joy.

Dear families, you know very well
that the true joy which we
experience in the family is not
superficial; it does not come from
material objects, from the fact that
everything seems to be going
well….True joy comes from a
profound harmony between
persons, something which we all
feel in our hearts and which makes
us experience the beauty of
togetherness, of mutual support
along life's journey.

The basis of this feeling of deep joy is the presence of God, the presence of God in the family and his love, which is welcoming, merciful, and respectful toward all.

The family that experiences the joy of faith communicates it naturally. That family is the salt of the earth and the light of the world, it is the leaven of society as a whole.

Joy is the sign that our hearts have
found what is good for them. But
the ultimate good for our hearts
does not consist in our domination
of any situation; it does not consist
in controlling what is done or said
around us or even what happens
within us. Our ultimate good lies in
our love for concrete persons.

The joy of the Gospel is such that
it cannot be taken away from
us by anyone or anything
(cf. John 16:22). The evils of our
world—and those of the Church—
must not be excuses for
diminishing our commitment
and our fervor. Let us look upon
them as challenges which
can help us to grow.

As disciples, we produce light that provokes joy, and from the joy flows glory. This is the essence of bearing testimony: stirring praise and adoration of the Father through the joy that invades the hearts of those who see and hear the message.

It is the joy we each have when we discover the closeness and the presence of Jesus in our life; a presence which transforms our existence and makes us open to the needs of our brothers and sisters, a presence which prompts us to welcome every other presence, even that of the foreigner and the immigrant.

You, dear young people, let no one steal your hope! I've said it many times, and I will repeat it once more: don't let them steal your hope! Adoring Jesus in your hearts and staying united with him, you will know how to stand up to evil, to injustice, and to violence with the strength of goodness, honesty, and virtue.

Jesus has awakened great hopes,
especially in the hearts of the
simple, the humble, the poor,
the forgotten, those who do not
matter in the eyes of the world.
He understands human sufferings,
he has shown the face of God's
mercy, and he has bent down to
heal body and soul.

Dear friends, if we walk in hope, allowing ourselves to be surprised by the new wine which Jesus offers us, we have joy in our hearts and we cannot fail to be witnesses of this joy. Christians are joyful, they are never gloomy.

Every Christian, and especially you
and I, is called to be a bearer of this
message of hope that gives serenity
and joy: God's consolation, his
tenderness toward all.

Hope is the virtue of those who, experiencing conflict—the struggle between life and death, good and evil—believe in the resurrection of Christ, in the victory of love.

Anyone who is a man or a woman
of hope—the great hope which
faith gives us—knows that even in
the midst of difficulties, God acts
and he surprises us.

Today too, amid so much darkness, we need to see the light of hope and to be men and women who bring hope to others. To protect creation, to protect every man and every woman, to look upon them with tenderness and love is to open up a horizon of hope; it is to let a shaft of light break through the heavy clouds; it is to bring the warmth of hope!

How many difficulties in married
life are resolved when we leave
room for dreaming, when we stop a
moment to think of our spouse,
and we dream about the goodness
present in the good things
all around us?

To remember what God has done and continues to do for me, for us, to remember the road we have travelled; this is what opens our hearts to hope for the future. May we learn to remember everything that God has done in our lives.

The joy of evangelizing always arises from grateful remembrance: it is a grace which we constantly need to implore. The apostles never forgot the moment when Jesus touched their hearts. The believer is essentially "one who remembers."

God always saves the best for us.
But he asks us to let ourselves
be surprised by his love,
to accept his surprises.

True joy does not come from things or from possessing, no! It is born from the encounter, from the relationship with others; it is born from feeling accepted, understood, and loved, and from accepting, from understanding, and from loving; and this is not because of a passing fancy but because the other is a person.

Joy is born from the gratuitousness of an encounter! It is hearing someone say, but not necessarily with words, "You are important to me." This is beautiful….And it is these very words that God makes us understand. In calling you, God says to you, "You are important to me, I love you, I am counting on you."

May

Church as Home and Mother

Women

Motherhood

She gets up while it is still dark;
she provides food for her family
….She sets about her work vigor-
ously; her arms are strong for her
tasks.

Proverbs 31:15–17

The Church that cares for children
and the elderly becomes the
mother of generations of believers
and, at the same time, serves
human society because a spirit of
love, familiarity, and solidarity
helps all people to rediscover
the fatherhood and
motherhood of God.

A Church without women is
like the college of the Apostles
without Mary....But think about it.
Our Lady is more important than
the Apostles! She is more
important!

The Church is a mother in that she
preaches in the same way that a
mother speaks to her child,
knowing that the child trusts that
what she is teaching is for his
or her benefit, for children know
that they are loved. Moreover, a
good mother can recognize
everything that God is bringing
about in her children; she listens
to their concerns and
learns from them.

The Church without frontiers, Mother to all, spreads throughout the world a culture of acceptance and solidarity, in which no one is seen as useless, out of place, or disposable. When living out this motherhood effectively, the Christian community nourishes, guides, and indicates the way, accompanying all with patience, and drawing close to them through prayer and works of mercy.

The Church acknowledges the indispensable contribution which women make to society through the sensitivity, intuition, and other distinctive skill sets which they, more than men, tend to possess. I think, for example, of the special concern which women show to others, which finds a particular, even if not exclusive, expression in motherhood.

The Church, beyond being a community of the faithful that sees the face of Jesus Christ in its neighbor, is a Mother without limits and without frontiers. She is the Mother of all and so she strives to foster the culture of welcome and solidarity, where no one is considered useless, out of place, or disposable.

The Church is the home where the doors are always open, not only because everyone finds a welcome and is able to breathe in love and hope, but also because we can go out bearing this love and this hope.

In this, her motherhood, the Church has as its model the Virgin Mary, the highest and most beautiful model that can be. The first Christian communities have already highlighted this, and the Second Vatican Council expressed it in an admirable way.

The Church is our mother because she has delivered us in Baptism. Whenever a child is baptized, he becomes a son of the Church; from that day, he is in the Church which cares for him as a caring mother, she makes us grow in faith and shows us, with the power of the Word of God, the way of salvation, defending us from evil.

The Church has received from
Jesus the precious treasure of the
Gospel, not to keep it for herself,
but giving it generously to others—
as a mother does. In this service of
evangelization, the maternity of the
Church is shown in a particular
way—committed, as a mother,
offering her children the spiritual
nourishment that feeds and makes
fruitful the Christian life.

The mother Church, she gives her children this word, raising us throughout our whole life with this word. And this is great; it's mother Church who, with this word, really changes us from the inside. The words that mother Church gives us transform us, making our humanity beat not according to the flesh but according to the Spirit.

In her motherly care, the
Church strives to show believers
the way to go to live a fruitful
existence of joy and peace.

The Church is a woman! The Church is a mother! And that's beautiful! We have to think deeply about this.

Dear friends, this is the Church: this is the Church that we all love, the Church that I love. A mother who has at heart the welfare of their children, that has the capacity to give life to her children.

Mary's motherhood is certainly unique, singular, and was accomplished in the fullness of time, when the Virgin gave birth to the Son of God, conceived by the Holy Spirit.

She [Mary], who cared for her divine Son, who propitiated his first miracle at the wedding at Cana, who was present on Calvary and at the Pentecost, shows you the road to take to deepen the meaning and role of women in society and to be fully faithful to the Lord Jesus Christ and to your mission in the world.

The first thing that she
(the Virgin Mary) did when she
received the Good News in her
womb was to run out to serve.
Let us run out to serve by bringing
to others the Good News that we
believe in. May this be our
conversion: the Good News of
Christ yesterday, today, and always.

Many women share pastoral
responsibilities with priests,
helping to guide people, families,
and groups and offering new
contributions to theological
reflection. But we need to create
still broader opportunities
for a more incisive female
presence in the Church.

The feminine genius is needed in
all expressions in the life of society;
the presence of women must also
be guaranteed in the workplace
and in the various other settings
where important decisions are
made, both in the Church and
in social structures.

Demands that the legitimate rights
of women be respected, based on
the firm conviction that men and
women are equal in dignity,
present the Church with
profound and challenging
questions which cannot
be lightly evaded.

I think of the steadfast faith of those mothers tending their sick children who, though perhaps barely familiar with the articles of the creed, cling to a rosary; or of all the hope poured into a candle lighted in a humble home with a prayer for help from Mary, or in the gaze of tender love directed to Christ crucified.

Doubly poor are those women who endure situations of exclusion, mistreatment, and violence, since they are frequently less able to defend their rights. Even so, we constantly witness among them impressive examples of daily heroism in defending and protecting their vulnerable families.

The first witnesses of the birth of Jesus were shepherds—simple, humble people; the first witnesses of the Resurrection were women. And this is beautiful. This is part of the mission of women, of mothers—witnessing to their children and to their grandchildren that Jesus is alive…and is risen. Mothers and women, carry on witnessing to this!

A mother defends herself with a heart filled with love before doing so with words. I wonder whether there is any love for the Church in the hearts of those who pay so much attention to the scandals.

As when a mother takes her child
upon her knee and caresses
him or her, so the Lord will
do and does with us.

Many things can change and have changed in our cultural and social evolution, but the fact remains that it is the woman who conceives, carries in her womb, and gives birth...this is not simply a biological matter, but carries... implications for the woman herself, for her way of being, for her relationships, for the way in which we lend respect to human life and to life in general.

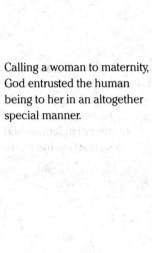

Calling a woman to maternity,
God entrusted the human
being to her in an altogether
special manner.

I would like to stress that woman
has a particular sensitivity to the
"things of God," above all in
helping us understand
the mercy, tenderness, and
love that God has for us.

It is in dialogue with God,
enlightened by prayer, that the
Christian woman continually
searches to answer the Lord's call
in the reality of her situation.

The family comes alive as it
reaches beyond itself; families
who do so communicate their
message of life and communion,
giving comfort and hope to more
fragile families, and thus build up
the Church herself, which is
the family of families.

In the Church, and in the journey of faith, women have had and still have a special role in opening doors to the Lord.

June

God's Family

God's Love and Mercy

God's Word

We love because God first loved us.

1 John 4:19

What is God's plan? It is to make of us all a single family of his children, in which each person feels that God is close and feels loved by him, as in the Gospel parable, feels the warmth of being God's family.

Faith is a gift and an act which
concerns us personally, but God
calls us to live our faith together,
as a family, as Church.

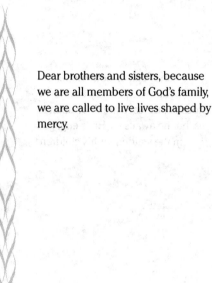

Dear brothers and sisters, because we are all members of God's family, we are called to live lives shaped by mercy.

We can speak of God's hope: our Father expects us always, he doesn't just leave the door open to us, but he awaits us. He is engaged in the waiting for his children.

There are no difficulties, trials, or misunderstandings to fear, provided we remain united to God as branches to the vine, provided we do not lose our friendship with him, provided we make ever more room for him in our lives.

Above all, a love which is patient: patience is a virtue of God and he teaches us how to cultivate it in family life, how to be patient, and lovingly so, with each other....God alone knows how to create harmony from differences. But if God's love is lacking, the family loses its harmony, self-centeredness prevails, and joy fades.

God is the Living One, the Merciful
One; Jesus brings us the life of God;
the Holy Spirit gives and keeps us
in our new life as true sons and
daughters of God.

The Lord is a Father and he says
that he will be for us like a
mother with her baby, with a
mother's tenderness.

No one adores one who doesn't love; no one adores one they do not consider to be their love. We are lovers! God is love! This certainty is what leads us to worship with all our heart the one who "loved us first" (1 John 4:10).

Rather than being a distant deity, God is the Father who accompanies all growth; he is the daily bread that nourishes; he is the merciful one who is near at hand in the moments when the enemy would exploit his children.

We are called to walk in order to
enter ever more deeply into the
mystery of the love of God, which
reigns over us and permits us to live
in serenity and hope.

Come to me, families from around the world—Jesus says—and I will give you rest, so that your joy may be complete. Take home this Word of Jesus, carry it in your hearts, share it with the family. It invites us to come to Jesus so that he may give this joy to us and to everyone.

The Bible, not to place it on a shelf,
but to keep it at hand, to read it
often, every day, both individually
and together, husband and wife,
parents and children, maybe in the
evening, especially on Sundays.
This way the family grows, walks
with the light and power of the
Word of God!

The Gospel...the message of
salvation, has two destinations that
are connected: the first, to awaken
faith, and this is evangelization; the
second, to transform the world
according to God's plan, and this is
the Christian animation of society.
But these are not two separate
things, they form one mission:
to carry the Gospel by the
witness of our lives in order to
transform the world!

Contact with the Word of God draws us near to the Kingdom of God. Consider this: a small Gospel always at hand, ready to open when the opportunity arises, ready to read what Jesus says; Jesus is there.

God's Word teaches that our brothers and sisters are the prolongation of the incarnation for each of us: "As you did it to one of these, the least of my brethren, you did it to me" (Matt 25:40).

The Word of God has creative force,
and once God speaks a word to us,
it can only become Word made
flesh.

To receive the gift of the Word made flesh, we must hear it from our fleshly neediness, from our wounds, from our own debility. Otherwise, the flesh would wax proud. That is why the Lord comes for the sake of the sickly and not the healthy; that is why he heals our frail flesh and becomes food to nourish it. Only by the flesh of Christ do we reach the Word.

The study of the Sacred Scriptures
must be a door opened to every
believer. Evangelization demands
familiarity with God's Word.

In the being and vocation of
every Christian is the personal
encounter with the Lord.
To seek God is to seek his face,
to enter into his intimacy.

No single act of love for God will be lost, no generous effort is meaningless, no painful endurance is wasted.

The Church needs us also to be
peacemakers, building peace
by our words, our hopes,
and our prayers.

The compassion of the Gospel is
that which accompanies in times of
need, that is, the compassion of the
Good Samaritan, who "sees,"
"has compassion," approaches,
and provides concrete help
(cf. Luke 10:33).

Let us learn to rest in the
tenderness of the arms of
the Father amid our creative and
generous commitment. Let us keep
marching forward; let us give
him everything, allowing him
to make our efforts bear
fruit in his good time.

All of creation forms a harmonious
and good unity, but above all
humanity, made in the image and
likeness of God, is one family,
in which relationships are marked
by a true fraternity not only in
words: the other person is a
brother or sister to love.

In our way of faith, it is also important to know and to feel that God loves us and not to be afraid to love him. Faith is professed with the lips and with the heart, with words and with love.

We are confronted with two rival
projects. The first is the project of
our faith that recognizes God as
Father; this is the project that works
for justice and makes us all
brothers and sisters. The other
project is the one proposed to us
by the enemy acting as an angel of
light; it is the project of the absent
God, where humans prey on
humans and the law of the
strongest prevails. Which project
will I choose?

God offers us this time with mercy
and patience so that we may learn
every day to recognize him in the
poor and in the lowly. Let us strive
for goodness and be watchful in
prayer and in love. May the Lord, at
the end of our life and at the end of
history, be able to recognize us as
good and faithful servants.

In the Bible, God always appears as the one who takes the initiative in the encounter with man: it is he who seeks man, and usually he seeks him precisely while man is in the bitter and tragic moment of betraying God and fleeing from him. God does not wait in seeking him; he seeks him out immediately.

This is God's way of doing things: he is not impatient like us, who often want everything all at once, even in our dealings with other people. God is patient with us because he loves us, and those who love are able to understand, to hope, to inspire confidence; they do not give up, they do not burn bridges, they are able to forgive.

July

Celebrate Life
Respect for Life
Human Dignity
Creation

And God blessed them. And God said to them, "Be fruitful and multiply and fill the earth and subdue it and have dominion over the fish of the sea and over the birds of the heavens and over every living thing that moves on the earth."

Genesis 1:28

July

And God blessed them. And God said
to them, Be fruitful, and multiply, and
fill the earth and subdue it; and have
dominion over the fish of the sea and
over the birds of the heavens, and over
every living thing that moves on the
earth.

Genesis 1:28

To assist the poor is good and
necessary, but it is not enough. I
encourage you to multiply your
efforts in the area of human
promotion, so that every man and
every woman can know the joy
which comes from the dignity of
earning their daily bread and
supporting their family.

The unemployed, whether men or
women, must also sense the dignity
which comes from providing for
their household, of being
breadwinners!

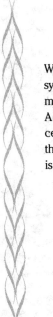

We are in a world economic
system which is centered on
money, not on the human person.
A genuine economic system is
centered on man and woman,
the human person. Today, money
is at the center.

Work is part of God's loving plan;
we are called to cultivate and care
for all the goods of creation and,
in this way, share in the
work of creation!

Work is fundamental to the dignity of a person. Work, to use a metaphor, "anoints" us with dignity, fills us with dignity, makes us similar to God, who has worked and still works, who always acts (cf. John 5:17); it gives one the ability to maintain oneself, one's family, to contribute to the growth of one's own nation.

Every human being is a child of
God! He or she bears the image
of Christ! We ourselves need
to see, and then to enable others
to see, that migrants and refugees
do not only represent a problem to
be solved, but are brothers and
sisters to be welcomed,
respected, and loved.

A change of attitude toward
migrants and refugees is needed on
the part of everyone, moving away
from attitudes of defensiveness
and fear, indifference and
marginalization—all typical of a
throwaway culture—toward
attitudes based on a culture of
encounter, the only culture capable
of building a better, more just,
and fraternal world.

Poor health and disability are never
a good reason for excluding or,
worse, for eliminating a person;
and the most serious privation that
elderly persons undergo is not the
weakening of the body and the
disability that may ensue, but
abandonment and exclusion,
the privation of love.

A society truly welcomes life when it recognizes that it is also precious in old age, in disability, in serious illness, and even when it is fading; when it teaches that the call to human fulfillment does not exclude suffering; indeed, when it teaches its members to see in the sick and suffering a gift for the entire community, a presence that summons them to solidarity and responsibility.

Violence against the elderly is inhuman, just as that against children. But God does not abandon you; he is with you! With his help you are and you continue to be the memory for your people, as well as for us, for the great family of the Church.

Having Sundays free from work—apart from necessary services—stands to confirm that the priority is not economic but human, gratuitousness, not business relationships but those of family, of friends, for believers the relationship with God and with the community.

Let us ask the Lord to show us and
the world the beauty and fullness
of this new life, of being born of the
Spirit, of treating each other with
kindness, with respect. Let us ask
for this grace for us all.

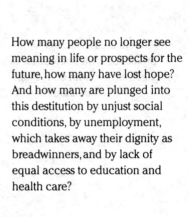

How many people no longer see meaning in life or prospects for the future, how many have lost hope? And how many are plunged into this destitution by unjust social conditions, by unemployment, which takes away their dignity as breadwinners, and by lack of equal access to education and health care?

Be sanctuaries of respect for life, proclaiming the sacredness of every human life from conception to natural death.

Whenever material things, money, worldliness, become the center of our lives, they take hold of us, they possess us; we lose our very identity as human beings.

A father knows all too well what it costs to hand down this heritage: how close, how gentle, and how firm to be. But what consolation and what recompense he receives when the children honor this legacy! It is a joy that rewards all the toil, that overcomes every misunderstanding, and heals every wound.

Let us focus on respect for others, looking especially at our attitude toward the young, since it is the parent–child or grandparent–grandchild relation that best reveals whether the older person has mastered a crisis or has fled from it.

There is no doubt that, in our time,
due to scientific and technical
advancements, the possibilities for
physical healing have significantly
increased; and yet, in some
respects it seems the capacity for
"taking care" of the person has
diminished, especially when
one is sick, frail, and helpless.

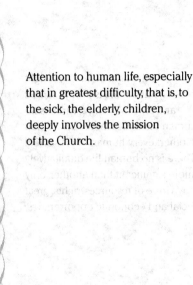

Attention to human life, especially
that in greatest difficulty, that is, to
the sick, the elderly, children,
deeply involves the mission
of the Church.

In the light of faith and right reason, human life is always sacred and always "quality." There is no human life that is more sacred than another: every human life is sacred! There is no human life qualitatively more significant than another, only by virtue of resources, rights, great social and economic opportunities.

Your work wants to witness by word
and by example that human life is
always sacred, valuable, and
inviolable. And as such, it must be
loved, defended, and cared for.

Fidelity to the Gospel of life and
respect for life as a gift from God
sometimes require choices that are
courageous and go against the
current, which in particular
circumstances, may become points
of conscientious objection.

Fathers must be patient. Often there is nothing else to do but wait; pray and wait with patience, gentleness, magnanimity, and mercy.

It is not "progressive" to try to resolve problems by eliminating a human life. On the other hand, it is also true that we have done little to adequately accompany women in very difficult situations, where abortion appears as a quick solution to their profound anguish, especially when the life developing within them is the result of rape or a situation of extreme poverty.

Appearances notwithstanding,
every person is immensely holy
and deserves our love.
Consequently, if I can help at least
one person to have a better life,
that already justifies the offering of
my life. It is a wonderful thing to be
God's faithful people. We achieve
fulfillment when we break down
walls and our heart is filled with
faces and names!

Homes for the elderly should be the "lungs" of humanity in a town, a neighborhood, or a parish. They should be the "sanctuaries" of humanity where one who is old and weak is cared for and protected like a big brother or sister.

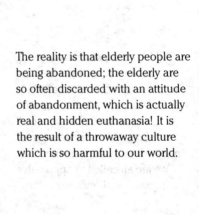

The reality is that elderly people are being abandoned; the elderly are so often discarded with an attitude of abandonment, which is actually real and hidden euthanasia! It is the result of a throwaway culture which is so harmful to our world.

Children are thrown away, young people are thrown away because they have no work, and the elderly are thrown away with the pretense of maintaining a "balanced" economy, which has at its center not the human person but money. We are all called to oppose this poisonous, throwaway culture!

Cultivating and caring for creation is an instruction of God which he gave not only at the beginning of history, but has also given to each one of us; it is part of his plan; it means making the world increase with responsibility, transforming it so that it may be a garden, an inhabitable place for us all.

Let us respect creation, let us not be instruments of destruction! Let us respect each human being. May there be an end to armed conflicts which cover the earth with blood; may the clash of arms be silenced; and everywhere may hatred yield to love, injury to pardon, and discord to unity.

A better world will come about
only if attention is first paid to
individuals; if human promotion is
integral, taking account of every
dimension of the person, including
the spiritual; if no one is neglected,
including the poor, the sick,
prisoners, the needy, and the
stranger (cf. Matt 25:31–46).

August

Human Family

*Family as Domestic Church
and School of Learning*

Love is patient and kind; love does not
envy or boast; it is not arrogant or rude.
It does not insist on its own way; it is
not irritable or resentful; it does not
rejoice at wrongdoing, but rejoices
with the truth. Love bears all things,
believes all things, hopes all things,
endures all things.

1 Corinthians 13:4–7

God wanted to be born into a
human family; he wanted to have a
mother and father like us.

I often think that a good indicator
for knowing how a family is doing
is seeing how their children
and elderly are treated.

The life of a family is filled with
beautiful moments: rest, meals
together, walks in the park or the
countryside, visits to grandparents
or to a sick person....But if love is
missing, if joy is missing, nothing is
fun. Jesus always gives us that love:
he is its endless source. In the
sacrament, he gives us his word and
he gives us the bread of life, so that
our joy may be complete.

In the family, the person becomes
aware of his or her own dignity
and, especially if their upbringing is
Christian, each one recognizes the
dignity of every single person, in a
particular way the sick, the weak,
and the marginalized.

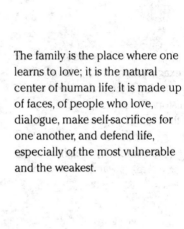

The family is the place where one learns to love; it is the natural center of human life. It is made up of faces, of people who love, dialogue, make self-sacrifices for one another, and defend life, especially of the most vulnerable and the weakest.

One could say, without exaggeration, that the family is the driving force of the world and of history. Our personality develops in the family, by growing up with our mom and dad, our brothers and sisters, by breathing in the warmth of the home.

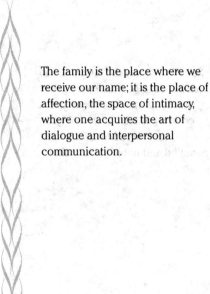

The family is the place where we receive our name; it is the place of affection, the space of intimacy, where one acquires the art of dialogue and interpersonal communication.

Sadly, in our day, the family all too often needs to be protected against insidious attacks and programs contrary to all that we hold true and sacred, all that is most beautiful and noble in our culture.

Making peace gives unity to the family; and tell young people, young couples, that it is not easy to go down this path, but it is a very beautiful path, very beautiful.

The "Good News" of the family
is a very important part of
evangelization, which Christians
can communicate to all by the
witness of their lives....This is
evident in secularized societies:
truly Christian families are known
by their fidelity, their patience, their
openness to life, and by
their respect for the elderly...the
secret to this is the presence of
Jesus in the family.

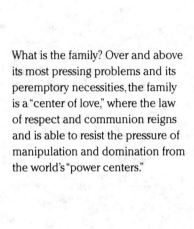

What is the family? Over and above its most pressing problems and its peremptory necessities, the family is a "center of love," where the law of respect and communion reigns and is able to resist the pressure of manipulation and domination from the world's "power centers."

In the heart of the family, the person naturally and harmoniously blends into a human group, overcoming the false opposition between the individual and society.

In the bosom of the family,
no one is set apart: both the elderly
and the child will be welcome
here. The culture of encounter and
of dialogue, openness to solidarity
and transcendence, originates in
the family.

This is a society of orphans....
Orphans, without the memory of
their families because, for example,
grandparents are far away or in a
retirement home, they don't have
that familial presence, that familial
memory. Orphans, without
affection today, or with a kind of
affection that is frantic: dad is tired,
mom is tired; they go to bed....
And they are left orphans.

We are called to acknowledge how beautiful, true, and good it is to start a family, to be a family today; and how indispensable the family is for the life of the world and for the future of humanity.

For the Christian community, the family is far more than a "theme": it is life, it is the daily fabric of life, it is the journey of generations who pass on the faith together with love and with the basic moral values. It is concrete solidarity, effort, patience, and also a project, hope, a future.

One of the most beautiful aspects of family life, of our human life as a family, is caressing a baby and being caressed by a grandfather and a grandmother.

Today's world, which is often
unhealthy because of secularism
and consumerism, seems
to be losing its ability to
celebrate and to live
as a family.

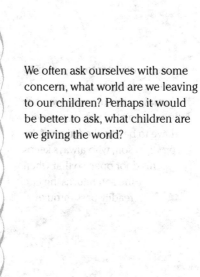

We often ask ourselves with some
concern, what world are we leaving
to our children? Perhaps it would
be better to ask, what children are
we giving the world?

Often it is better to stop rushing
from one thing to another and to
remain with someone who has
faltered along the way. At times we
have to be like the father of the
prodigal son, who always keeps
his door open so that when
the son returns, he can
readily pass through it.

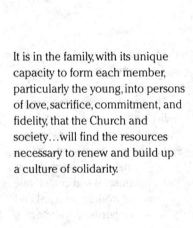

It is in the family, with its unique capacity to form each member, particularly the young, into persons of love, sacrifice, commitment, and fidelity, that the Church and society…will find the resources necessary to renew and build up a culture of solidarity.

The family is the privileged school
for learning generosity, sharing,
responsibility, a school that teaches
how to overcome a certain
individualistic mind-set which has
worked its way into our societies.
Sustaining and promoting families,
making the most of their
fundamental and central role
means working for a just and
supportive development.

Families are the domestic Church, where Jesus grows; he grows in the love of spouses, he grows in the lives of children.

I ask you especially to show concern for those who do not have a family of their own, in particular those who are elderly and children without parents. Never let them feel isolated, alone, and abandoned, but help them to know that God has not forgotten them.

The family…is the teacher of acceptance and solidarity: it is within the family that education substantially draws upon relationships of solidarity; in the family, one learns that the loss of health is not a reason for discriminating against human life; the family teaches us not to fall into individualism and to balance the "I" with the "we."

Over and over again, we see that family bonds are essential for the stability of relationships in society, for the work of education, and for integral human development; for they are inspired by love, responsible intergenerational solidarity, and mutual trust.

The spirit of love, which reigns in a family, guides both mother and child in their conversations; therein they teach and learn, experience correction, and grow in appreciation of what is good.

How do we keep our faith as a family? Do we keep it for ourselves in our families as a personal treasure like a bank account, or are we able to share it by our witness, by our acceptance of others, by our openness?

We all know that families, especially young families, are often "racing" from one place to another with lots to do. But did you ever think that this "racing" could also be the race of faith? Christian families are missionary families.

A family with no memory hardly deserves the name. A family that does not respect and attend to its grandparents, who are its memory, is a broken family; but a family and a people who remember are a family and a people with a future.

In your journey as a family, you share so many beautiful moments: meals, rest, housework, leisure, prayer, trips and pilgrimages, and times of mutual support.... Nevertheless, if there is no love then there is no joy, and authentic love comes to us from Jesus. He offers us his Word, which illuminates our path; he gives us the Bread of life which sustains us on our journey.

September

We Are Family

Heritage of Faith

Train up a child in the way he should go; even when he is old he will not depart from it.

Proverbs 22:6

Christian spouses are not naïve; they know life's problems and temptations. But they are not afraid to be responsible before God and before society. They do not run away, they do not hide; they do not shirk the mission of forming a family and bringing children into the world. But today, Father, it is difficult….Of course it is difficult!

Through their free and faithful act
of love, Christian spouses testify to
the fact that marriage, insofar as
it is a sacrament, is the foundation
of the family and strengthens
spousal union and the couple's
mutual gift of self.

It is normal for husband and wife to argue, it's normal. It always happens. But my advice is this: never let the day end without having first made peace. Never!

But be honest with me, how many times do you say thank you to your wife, and you to your husband? How many days go by without uttering this word, *thanks*?

Availability, the availability of a
father or mother to their children, is
so important: "spend time" with
your children, play with your
children.

I imagine how hectic the day of a dad or a mom is; they get up early, take their children to school, then they go to work, often in places where there are tensions and conflicts, as well as places that are far away.

The question stirs in our heart:
What can we do so that our
children, our kids, can give
meaning to their lives? Because
they also feel that our way of living
is sometimes inhuman, and they
do not know what direction to take
so that life can be beautiful and so
they're happy to get up in the
morning.

The many mothers and fathers who
make critical choices each day in
order to continue on with their
families, with their children…
are an example for us.

In the face of those moments of discouragement we experience in life, in our efforts to evangelize or to embody our faith as parents within the family, I would like to say forcefully, always know in your heart that God is by your side; he never abandons you! Let us never lose hope!

Jesus is the one who brings
together and unites generations!
He is the inexhaustible font of that
love which overcomes every
occasion of self-absorption,
solitude, and sadness.

In the Gospel, Jesus welcomes children, he embraces them and blesses them (cf. Mark 10:16). We too need to protect, guide, and encourage our young people, helping them to build a society worthy of their great spiritual and cultural heritage.

A good father knows how to wait
and knows how to forgive from the
depths of his heart. Certainly, he
also knows how to correct with
firmness: he is not a weak father,
submissive and sentimental. The
father who knows how to correct
without humiliating is the one who
knows how to protect without
sparing himself.

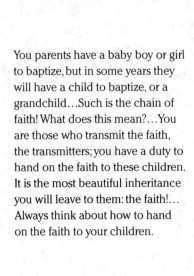

You parents have a baby boy or girl to baptize, but in some years they will have a child to baptize, or a grandchild…Such is the chain of faith! What does this mean?…You are those who transmit the faith, the transmitters; you have a duty to hand on the faith to these children. It is the most beautiful inheritance you will leave to them: the faith!… Always think about how to hand on the faith to your children.

Today too, children are crying; they are crying a lot, and their crying challenges us. In a world which daily discards tons of food and medicine, there are children, hungry and suffering from easily curable diseases, who cry out in vain.

In an age which insists on the protection of minors, there is a flourishing trade in weapons which end up in the hands of child-soldiers; there is a ready market for goods produced by the slave labor of small children.

When families bring children into
the world, train them in faith and
sound values, and teach them to
contribute to society, they become
a blessing in our world.

I find there are three paths for young people, for children, and little ones: the path of education, the path of sports, and the path of work, when there are jobs for young people to start with!

So many young people spend their lives spaced out on drugs and noise because they have no direction, because no one told them that there was something great!

We must encounter our faith, the
faith of our fathers and mothers,
which is liberating in itself without
any added quality or qualification.
In the moment of making concrete
decisions, this faith will lead us
through the Spirit's anointing,
to a clear knowledge of the limits
of our own role; it will make us
wise and intelligent in choosing
the means we use.

Look upon your brother's sorrow—
I think of the children: look upon
these…look at the sorrow of your
brother, stay your hand and do not
add to it, rebuild the harmony that
has been shattered; and all this
achieved not by conflict but by
encounter! May the noise of
weapons cease!

We Christians are called to confront the poverty of our brothers and sisters, to touch it, to make it our own, and to take practical steps to alleviate it.

Do you listen to your grandparents? Do you open your hearts to the memories that your grandparents pass on? Grandparents are like the wisdom of the family, they are the wisdom of a people. And a people that does not listen to grandparents is one that dies! Listen to your grandparents.

A grandfather is a father twice over
and a grandmother is a mother
twice over.

Grandparents, who have received
the blessing to see their children's
children (cf. Ps 128:6), are
entrusted with a great
responsibility: to transmit their life
experience, their family history,
the history of a community, of a
people; to share wisdom with
simplicity, and the faith itself—
the most precious heritage!
Happy is the family who have
grandparents close by!

Let us pray for our grandfathers
and grandmothers who often
played a heroic role in handing on
the faith in times of persecution.
Especially in times past, when
fathers and mothers often were not
at home or had strange ideas,
confused as they were by the
fashionable ideologies of the day,
grandmothers were the ones who
handed on the Faith.

The elderly pass on history,
doctrine, faith, and they leave them
to us as an inheritance. They are
like a fine vintage wine; that is, they
have within themselves the power
to give us this noble inheritance.

A society that neglects children
and marginalizes the elderly severs
its roots and darkens its future.

Every time a child is abandoned
and an elderly person cast out,
not only is it an act of injustice,
but it also ensures the failure
of that society.

Caring for our little ones and for our elders is a choice for civilization. And also for the future, because the little ones, the children, the young people will carry society forward by their strength, their youth, and the elderly people will carry it forward by their wisdom, their memory, which they must give to us all.

The care given to the elderly, like
that of children, is an indicator of
the quality of a community.

October

Family Values

Listening and Dialogue

Listen, my son, to your father's instruction and do not forsake your mother's teaching.

Proverbs 1:8

Saying "thank you" is such an easy
thing, and yet so hard! How often
do we say "thank you" to one
another in our families? These are
essential words for our life in
common: "sorry," "excuse me,"
"thank you." If families can say
these three things, they will be fine.

In the light of God's Word, I would
like to ask you, dear families, do
you pray together from time to time
as a family? Some of you do,
I know. But so many people say
to me, but how can we?

Why do we not try to live and pass on the priority of nonquantifiable values: friendship (so dear, this time in the best sense of the word, to our teenagers!), the ability to celebrate and simply enjoy the good times,… sincerity, which produces peace and trust, and the confidence that encourages sincerity?

Children need to find a father waiting for them when they come home after failing. They will do everything not to admit it, not to show it, but they need it; and not to find it opens wounds in them that are difficult to heal.

Our personal experience of being accompanied and assisted, and of openness to those who accompany us, will teach us to be patient and compassionate with others, and to find the right way to gain their trust, their openness, and their readiness to grow.

Together with young people everywhere, you want to help build a world where we all live together in peace and friendship, overcoming barriers, healing divisions, rejecting violence and prejudice. And this is exactly what God wants for us.

He who becomes a friend of God
loves his brothers and sisters,
commits himself to safeguarding
their life and their health, and also
to respecting the environment
and nature.

And also praying for one another!
The husband for his wife, the wife
for her husband, both together for
their children, the children for their
grandparents....praying for each
other. This is what it means to pray
in the family, and it is what makes
the family strong: prayer.

We all make mistakes and on occasion someone gets offended in the marriage, in the family, and sometimes—I say—plates are smashed, harsh words are spoken, but please listen to my advice: don't ever let the sun set without reconciling. Peace is made each day in the family: "Please forgive me," and then you start over.

To care for individuals and peoples in need means protecting memory and hope; it means taking responsibility for the present with its situations of utter marginalization and anguish and being capable of bestowing dignity upon it.

Fidelity is always personal: it has special names, codes, and gestures for every person. Persons are the highest value; above them, there is no higher realm of values.

Relationships based on faithful
love until death, like marriage,
fatherhood, being child or sibling,
are learned and lived in the
household. When these
relationships form the basic fabric
of a human society, they lend
cohesion and consistency.

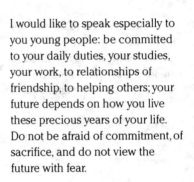

I would like to speak especially to you young people: be committed to your daily duties, your studies, your work, to relationships of friendship, to helping others; your future depends on how you live these precious years of your life. Do not be afraid of commitment, of sacrifice, and do not view the future with fear.

Are we ready to be there for children, to "waste time" with them? Are we ready to listen to them, to care for them, to pray for them and with them? Or do we ignore them because we are too caught up in our own affairs?

When a family loses the capacity to
dream, children do not grow, love
does not grow, life loses energy
and dies out.

The communion of life embraced by spouses, their openness to the gift of life, the mutual protection, the encounter and the memory of generations, educational support, the transmission of the Christian faith to their children....With all this, the family continues to be a school unparalleled in humanity, an indispensable contribution to a just and supportive society.

It becomes possible to build communion amid disagreement, but this can only be achieved by those great persons who are willing to go beyond the surface of the conflict and to see others in their deepest dignity.

We can speak of the faith of our ancestors, recalling the men and women who were the instruments God used to manifest his grace toward us. We can also look into the future and envision our own spiritual descendants, those who will receive our mission and our testimony about this revelation.

We need to be convinced that charity "is the principle not only of micro-relationships (with friends, with family members, or within small groups) but also of macro-relationships (social, economic, and political ones)."

Without love, no gift or charism
could serve the Church, for where
there is not love there is an
emptiness that becomes
filled with selfishness.

In God's great plan, every detail is important, even yours, even my humble little witness, even the hidden witness of those who live their faith with simplicity in everyday family relationships, work relationships, friendships. They are the saints of every day.

We need to practice the art of
listening which is more than
simply hearing. Listening, in
communication, is an openness of
heart which makes possible that
closeness without which genuine
spiritual encounter cannot occur.
Listening helps us to find the right
gesture and word which shows
that we are more than
simply bystanders.

The culture of encounter and of dialogue, openness to solidarity and transcendence, originates in the family.

Let us pray, then, for the emergence
of new opportunities for dialogue,
encounter and the resolution of
differences, for continued
generosity in providing
humanitarian assistance to
those in need, and for an
ever-greater recognition that all…
are brothers and sisters, members
of one family, one people.

Those who listen in a healthy way can transform personal ties, which were so often hurtful, with the simple balm of acknowledging that the other is important and has something to say to me. Listening fosters dialogue and makes possible the miracle of empathy that overcomes distance and resentments.

Listening is more than hearing.
Hearing is related to information.
But the first thing about real
communication is the heart's ability
to make nearness possible; without
this, there can be no authentic
encounter. Listening helps us to
find the timely gesture and word
that draw us out of the always more
comfortable condition of spectator.

To listen is to care for, understand,
value, respect, and save what others
say. We need the means to listen
well, so that all may speak and so
that what each person wants to
say is taken into account.

To dialogue is to be attentive to the Word of God and to let ourselves be asked questions by him; to dialogue is to proclaim his Good News and also to know how to sound out the questions, the doubts, the sufferings, and hopes of our brothers and sisters whom we accompany and acknowledge as our companions and guides on the journey.

The exercise of constructive
dialogue is the most human way
of communicating. In all areas,
space for serious, constructive,
and not merely formal dialogue
should be established.

It takes so much patience to do this: to be a good parent, a good grandfather, a good mother, a good grandmother. It takes so much patience and with this patience comes holiness by exercising patience.

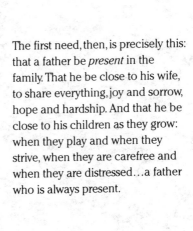

The first need, then, is precisely this: that a father be *present* in the family. That he be close to his wife, to share everything, joy and sorrow, hope and hardship. And that he be close to his children as they grow: when they play and when they strive, when they are carefree and when they are distressed...a father who is always present.

November

Mission and Witness

Call and Vocation

Evangelization

Love never ends. As for prophecies, they will pass away; as for tongues, they will cease; as for knowledge, it will pass away.

1 Corinthians 13:8

The witness of the family is crucial, before the whole of society, in reaffirming the importance of an elderly person as a member of a community, who has his or her own mission to accomplish, and who only seemingly receives with nothing to offer.

Our true vocation is to be a faithful
and wise steward whom the Lord
has put in charge of his household
to give others the nourishment
they need at the proper time.

I would ask you, as families, to be especially mindful of our call to be missionary disciples of Jesus. This means being ready to go beyond your homes and to care for our brothers and sisters who are most in need.

My mission of being in the heart
of the people is not just a part of
my life or a badge I can take off;
it is not an "extra" or just another
moment in life. Instead, it
is something I cannot uproot
from my being without
destroying my very self.

Only by becoming poor ourselves, by stripping away our complacency, will we be able to identify with the least of our brothers and sisters. We will see things in a new light and thus respond with honesty and integrity to the challenge of proclaiming the radicalism of the Gospel in a society which has grown comfortable with social exclusion, polarization, and scandalous inequality.

Sometimes we lose our enthusiasm for mission because we forget that the Gospel responds to our deepest needs, since we were created for what the Gospel offers us: friendship with Jesus and love of our brothers and sisters.

I encourage all of you to witness to concrete solidarity with brothers and sisters, especially those who are most in need of justice, hope, and tenderness.

Where does Jesus send us? There are no borders, no limits: he sends us to everyone....The Lord seeks all, he wants everyone to feel the warmth of his mercy and his love.

Do you know what the best tool is
for evangelizing the young?
Another young person!

People today certainly need words, but most of all they need us to bear witness to the mercy and tenderness of the Lord, which warms the heart, rekindles hope, and attracts people toward the good.

Each individual Christian and every community is missionary to the extent that they bring to others and live the Gospel, and testify to God's love for all, especially those experiencing difficulties. Be missionaries of God's love and tenderness! Be missionaries of God's mercy, which always forgives us, always awaits us, and loves us dearly.

Our vocation would not be full if it excluded our mud, our falls, our failures, our daily struggles; in fragility, the life of Christ manifests itself and becomes a saving proclamation.

As disciples, we are promised the Spirit of truth who will bear witness, who will teach us all things, and who will lead us to the fullness of truth. In our docility to the Holy Spirit, the source of all revelation, we have the assurance of receiving and transmitting the revelation of Christ rather than a merely human message.

There is nothing improvised in this
following of Jesus—it requires the
preparation of a lifetime.

All of us are called to offer others
an explicit witness to the saving
love of the Lord, who despite our
imperfections offers us his
closeness, his Word and his
strength, and gives meaning
to our lives.

I am a mission on this earth; that is
the reason why I am here in this
world. We have to regard ourselves
as sealed, even branded, by this
mission of bringing light, blessing,
enlivening, rising up, healing,
and freeing.

The new evangelization calls for personal involvement on the part of each of the baptized. Every Christian is challenged, here and now, to be actively engaged in evangelization; indeed, anyone who has truly experienced God's saving love does not need much time or lengthy training to go out and proclaim that love.

Christians have the duty to proclaim the Gospel without excluding anyone. Instead of seeming to impose new obligations, they should appear as people who wish to share their joy, who point to a horizon of beauty, and who invite others to a delicious banquet. It is not by proselytizing that the Church grows.

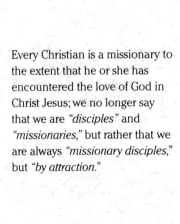

Every Christian is a missionary to the extent that he or she has encountered the love of God in Christ Jesus; we no longer say that we are *"disciples"* and *"missionaries,"* but rather that we are always *"missionary disciples,"* but *"by attraction."*

Witnesses are the ones who have
seen something, and they want
to talk about it, describe it,
and communicate it.

Christ continues to call out to us, asking us to love and serve him by tending to our brothers and sisters in need.

Let us encourage the generosity
which is typical of the young and
help them to work actively in
building a better world. Young
people are a powerful engine for
the Church and for society.

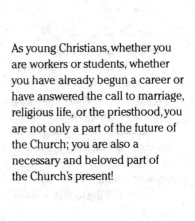

As young Christians, whether you are workers or students, whether you have already begun a career or have answered the call to marriage, religious life, or the priesthood, you are not only a part of the future of the Church; you are also a necessary and beloved part of the Church's present!

In giving us a mission, the Lord grounds us; he gives us a solid foundation. And he does not do so with the perfunctory attitude of someone giving us an ordinary task to perform, but with the empowering might of his Spirit, so that our identity is sealed by the very way in which we are made to belong to that mission.

Even when many of our brothers
and sisters do not profess our
Creed, it remains essential that we
do—essential for us and for them,
although they can't see it, provided
that through this journey we will be
collaborating in the coming of the
Kingdom for all, even for those who
have been unable to recognize it in
the ecclesial signs.

Laypeople are, put simply, the vast majority of the people of God. The minority—ordained ministers—are at their service. There has been a growing awareness of the identity and mission of the laity in the Church. The formation of the laity and the evangelization of professional and intellectual life represent a significant pastoral challenge.

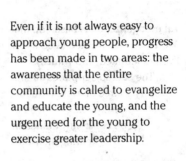

Even if it is not always easy to approach young people, progress has been made in two areas: the awareness that the entire community is called to evangelize and educate the young, and the urgent need for the young to exercise greater leadership.

All evangelization is based on that
Word, listened to, meditated upon,
lived, celebrated, and witnessed to.
The Sacred Scriptures are the
very source of evangelization.
Consequently, we need to
be constantly trained in
hearing the Word.

The primary reason for
evangelizing is the love of Jesus
which we have received, the
experience of salvation which
urges us to ever greater love of him.
What kind of love would not feel
the need to speak of the beloved,
to point him out, to make him
known?

Am I really my brother's keeper?
Yes, you are your brother's keeper!
To be human means to care for
one another! But when harmony
is broken, a metamorphosis
occurs: the brother who is to be
cared for and loved becomes an
adversary to fight, to kill.

December

Holy Family

Holy Spirit

Good News

And I will be a father to you, and you shall be sons and daughters to me, says the Lord Almighty.

2 Corinthians 6:18

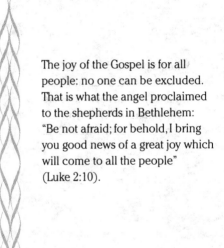

The joy of the Gospel is for all people: no one can be excluded. That is what the angel proclaimed to the shepherds in Bethlehem: "Be not afraid; for behold, I bring you good news of a great joy which will come to all the people" (Luke 2:10).

When a person discovers God, the true treasure, he abandons a selfish lifestyle and seeks to share with others the charity which comes from God.

The Gospel tells us constantly to run the risk of a face-to-face encounter with others, with their physical presence which challenges us, with their pain and their pleas, with their joy which infects us in our close and continuous interaction.

We know well that with Jesus life becomes richer and that with him it is easier to find meaning in everything. This is why we evangelize. A true missionary, who never ceases to be a disciple, knows that Jesus walks with him, speaks to him, breathes with him, works with him.

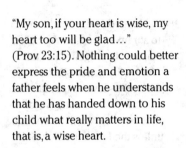

"My son, if your heart is wise, my heart too will be glad…" (Prov 23:15). Nothing could better express the pride and emotion a father feels when he understands that he has handed down to his child what really matters in life, that is, a wise heart.

How I long to find the right words
to stir up enthusiasm for a new
chapter of evangelization full of
fervor, joy, generosity, courage,
boundless love, and attraction!
Yet I realize that no words of
encouragement will be enough
unless the fire of the Holy Spirit
burns in our hearts.

December 7

A society without mothers would be a dehumanized society, for mothers are always, even in the worst moments, witnesses of tenderness, dedication, and moral strength.

[A person] is like a traveler who, crossing the deserts of life, thirsts for the living water: gushing and fresh, capable of quenching his deep desire for light, love, beauty, and peace. We all feel this desire!

Are you a parent or a grandparent?—Be a saint by passionately teaching your children or grandchildren to know and to follow Jesus.

It is certainly not difficult to imagine how much mothers could learn from Mary's care for that Son! And how much fathers could glean from the example of Joseph, a righteous man, who dedicated his life to supporting and protecting the Child and his wife—his family—in difficult times.

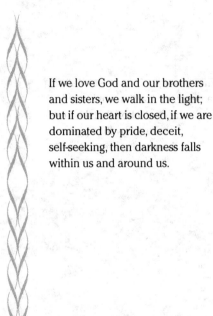

If we love God and our brothers
and sisters, we walk in the light;
but if our heart is closed, if we are
dominated by pride, deceit,
self-seeking, then darkness falls
within us and around us.

The message of peace is not about a negotiated settlement but rather the conviction that the unity brought by the Spirit can harmonize every diversity.

Saint Joseph was not stubborn in following his own life plans; he did not allow resentment to poison his soul, but he was prepared to make himself disposed to the news that, in a disconcerting way, was presented to him....

When the Spirit causes us to be
born to new life, he makes us
gentle and kind, not judgmental:
the only Judge is the Lord....If I
have something to say, let me say it
to the individual, not to the entire
neighborhood; only to the one
who can remedy the situation.

Let us ask the Holy Spirit *to anoint* our whole being with the oil of his mercy, which heals the injuries caused by mistakes, misunderstandings, and disputes. And let us ask him for the grace to send us forth, in humility and meekness, along the demanding but enriching path of seeking peace.

Let us believe the Gospel when it tells us that the kingdom of God is already present in this world and is growing, here and there, and in different ways: like the small seed which grows into a great tree (cf. Matt 13:31–32), like the measure of leaven that makes the dough rise (cf. Matt 13:33), and like the good seed that grows amid the weeds (cf. Matt 13:24–30) and can always pleasantly surprise us.

Throughout the history of salvation, whenever God reveals himself, he brings newness—God always brings newness—and demands our complete trust.

Let us open the doors to the Spirit,
let ourselves be guided by him, and
allow God's constant help to make
us new men and women, inspired
by the love of God which the
Holy Spirit bestows on us!

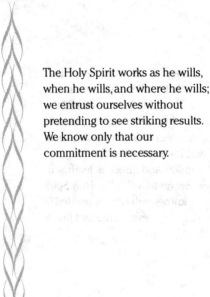

The Holy Spirit works as he wills,
when he wills, and where he wills;
we entrust ourselves without
pretending to see striking results.
We know only that our
commitment is necessary.

There is no greater freedom than that of allowing oneself to be guided by the Holy Spirit, renouncing the attempt to plan and control everything to the last detail, and instead letting him enlighten, guide, and direct us, leading us wherever he wills. The Holy Spirit knows well what is needed in every time and place.

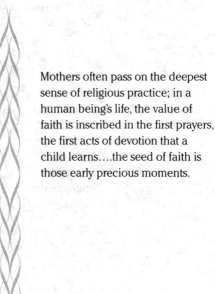

Mothers often pass on the deepest sense of religious practice; in a human being's life, the value of faith is inscribed in the first prayers, the first acts of devotion that a child learns....the seed of faith is those early precious moments.

True faith in the incarnate
Son of God is inseparable from
self-giving, from membership in
the community, from service, from
reconciliation with others.
The Son of God, by becoming
flesh, summoned us to the
revolution of tenderness.

Jesus, Mary, and Joseph knew what it meant to leave their own country and become migrants....But the maternal heart of Mary and the compassionate heart of Joseph, the Protector of the Holy Family, never doubted that God would always be with them. Through their intercession, may that same firm certainty dwell in the heart of every migrant and refugee.

Let us make ourselves ready to celebrate Christmas contemplating Mary and Joseph: Mary, the woman full of grace who had the courage to entrust herself fully to the Word of God; Joseph, the faithful and just man who chose to believe the Lord rather than listen to the voices of doubt and human pride.

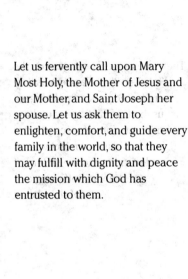

Let us fervently call upon Mary
Most Holy, the Mother of Jesus and
our Mother, and Saint Joseph her
spouse. Let us ask them to
enlighten, comfort, and guide every
family in the world, so that they
may fulfill with dignity and peace
the mission which God has
entrusted to them.

Therefore, as we fix our gaze on the Holy Family of Nazareth as they were forced to become refugees, let us think of the tragedy of those migrants and refugees who are victims of rejection and exploitation, who are victims of human trafficking and of slave labor.

The flight into Egypt caused by Herod's threat shows us that God is present where man is in danger, where man is suffering, where he is fleeing, where he experiences rejection and abandonment; but God is also present where man dreams, where he hopes to return in freedom to his homeland and plans and chooses life for his family and dignity for himself and his loved ones.

When Jesus came into the world,
his very life was threatened by a
corrupt king. Jesus himself needed
to be protected. He had an earthly
protector: Saint Joseph. He had an
earthly family: the Holy Family of
Nazareth. So he reminds us of the
importance of protecting our
families, and those larger families
which are the Church, God's family,
and the world, our human family.

Every human person owes his or her life to a mother and almost always owes much of what follows in life, both human and spiritual formation, to her.

Each Christian family can first of all—as Mary and Joseph did—welcome Jesus, listen to him, speak with him, guard him, protect him, grow with him; and in this way, improve the world. Let us make room in our heart and in our day for the Lord.

This is the great mission of the family: to make room for Jesus who is coming, to welcome Jesus in the family, in each member: children, husband, wife, grandparents.... Jesus is there.

Prayer for the
Year of the Family

Jesus, Mary, and Joseph,
in you we contemplate
the splendor of true love,
to you we turn with trust.

Holy Family of Nazareth,
grant that our families too
may be places of communion and prayer,
authentic schools of the Gospel
and small domestic Churches.

Holy Family of Nazareth,
may families never again
experience violence, rejection, and division:
may all who have been hurt or scandalized
find ready comfort and healing.

Holy Family of Nazareth,
may the approaching Synod of Bishops
make us once more mindful
of the sacredness and inviolability of the
        family,
and its beauty in God's plan.

Jesus, Mary, and Joseph,
graciously hear our prayer.
Amen.